Praise for *And Th*

"*And The Walls Came Tumbling* is a celebration and a warning. Darius Daughtry waxes nostalgic about the early days of hip-hop, first love, and family, while also naming the danger that is being black in America. "Anywhere could be where my black gets me dead," he writes. Here we find the pockets of joy to be found inside the sunshine state as well as the threat of violence that is as ever-present as the humidity. We find traditional forms, sonnets and odes, handled with precision, as well as a playlist turned into a poem and a golden shovel that would surely make Gwendolyn Brooks stand up and clap. This is a book that says poetry in Florida is alive and well."

- P. Scott Cunningham
Founder, O, Miami Poetry Festival and
Author, *Ya Te Veo* (University of Arkansas Press, 2018)

"In this powerful debut collection, Darius Daughtry shows us what it means to find God in the blues and in a grandmother's love, to find the truth behind what the world tells us about our Blackness and our personhood. In forms and free verse, and always with an eye toward rhythm, Daughtry's poetry cuts through the lies we're told and re-told. With these poems that shine an undimmable light, he makes the walls tumble."

- Ashley M. Jones
Author, *Magic City Gospel* and *dark // things*

AND THE WALLS CAME TUMBLING

Darius V. Daughtry

OMIOKUN BOOKS

And The Walls Came Tumbling

Copyright © 2019 by Darius V. Daughtry.

Cover illustration by Nathan "Nate Dee" Delinois.

All rights reserved.

Printed in the United States of America. No part of this book may be reproduced in any form or by any electronic or mechanical means, including information storage and retrieval systems, without written permission from the author, except for the use of brief quotations in a book review.

Omiokun Books
www.omiokunbooks.com

ISBN: 978-1-7335361-0-3
ISBN: 978-1-7335361-1-0 (ebook)

Gretchen,
You are a wonderful spirit & a beautiful poet. Keep giving of yourself.

for the breathless

Contents

P.E. and N.W.A. = ME   9
Darius, Can You Write Me A Poem?   13
Being   15
Hand Over Heart   18
That Time I Met Malcolm   19
Butterfly   21
Black Boys Fly   22
Lil' Man   23
Poetry is a One Hour Forty-Three Minute Playlist   26
Soul Brotha   27
Eric B. for President of the Deacon Board   30
Feel Jesus   32
Marvin's Mystique   34
For the Sun When Clouds Block Her Shine   39
Lying Feels Like Dying But Costs Less Than Caskets   40
It Just Makes Cents   43
ride the jam pony express or how to get dope boys to dance down South   44
Corner Store Sonnets   47
Everywhere Ain't For Everyone   49
That Daisy in the Dirt is Us   50
BSL Blues   51
Atlanta Pirates   53
what do ghosts smell like?   56
Jit   59
Odes to Little Black Boys Before They Don't Get the Chance to Become Black Men   61
Milk On Her Mouth 63
When I was Tina and Grandma was Ike   65
Sugar Water   67
You should write more _____ stuff, they say   69
Dae'kwon   70
Black Girl Wonderful   73
The Undying of Tamir Rice   76
I, Too, Am America and I'm Gone Sing/Aretha not Adele   78
And The Walls Came Tumbling   82

P.E. and N.W.A. = ME

I was born of *Fight the Power* & *Fuck the Police.*

But they try to beat *Don't Worry, Be Happy* into the brown boy.
Into the "don't move or make a sound, boy."
Into the 8 barrels pointed, 8 pins locked, 8 trigger fingers cocked,
"now, get on the ground, boy."

24/7
they try to remove my heart,
cut out the parts that beat rebel rhythms &
replace them with heaven, hope & hereafter hymns.
They try to sanctify me into submission
with songs of the sweet by & by
while in the here & now, Nina & Billie sing,
Strange Fruit swing like pendulum.
They say, "Don't fight.
It'll be alright when Jesus comes.
Just hum."

Hum…
        hum…
                hum…

When I was young,
somebody told me I was smart.
They tried to Stanford-Binet me into division,
Scantron score & diction the WE out of me.
They would have me believe I was better
because I got higher letters on my lessons.
Said I had the answers.
Didn't want me asking questions.

But I asked,
    What's Going On?
&

    Who's That Peeking in My Window?
When those that looked like me tried to sing,
they labeled them pitchy, said notes were off-key.

Softly they serenaded me with

    "you're not like the rest of them.
    Your voice is unique…be careful how you speak.
    Don't speak like them.their speech is all wrong.
    Don't drop those R's…don't sing their songs"

They wanted to pacify my P-Funk,
Kenny G my Coltrane.
Poor thangs,
don't they know
I come from queens,
kings,
& cotton-pickers?
Pocketbook carriers.
Pocket-knife next to bag of butterscotch in Sunday service.
Marvin & Mahalia Saturday morning singing while cleaning.
My grandma made sure my heart remained whole -
even when hers barely beat.
She sang me warrior –
    shaky voice.
She painted me king –
    strong hand.

I saw God daily in tattered housecoat & bedroom shoes.
Who knew God sang the blues
but kept rhythm tucked under her breast like
change had already come?

Sometimes all she had were those hums - wordless songs.
It was hard for Grandma to find a phrase like crack epidemic.
All she knew was that she lost both of her baby boys in it.
One, flicking a lighter to set fire to demons
dancing next to his shame.
The other, caught up when the allure of the game
kept calling his name.
This same old song keeps playing.
Pied Piper on repeat.
Hip-Hop switched up the beat for a while,
but it seems like we're back to that 1,2 step, smile.
That shuck & jive, grin real wide,
dance for Massa to stay alive &
throw your hands in the air like you just don't care,
like you just don't care,
like you just don't care.

How you just don't care?

Don't you know you were born of *FIGHT the power*?
You are the progeny of protest songs.
So, protest!
Resist!
No rest!
'Cause they ain't taking a break from breaking you down -
making you sound more like mumbles than chants.

This is your chance to get your song back.
Reclaim your birthright.
FIGHT!
FIGHT the power!
FIGHT the powers that be
until you find the power that beats inside your heart.
Don't let them cut out the parts that beat rebel rhythms.
'Cause complacency ain't got no groove.
Apathy don't you make you move.
But that fight –
that FIGHT gets you up out your seat.
That FIGHT rides the rhythm of the up & down beat.
That FIGHT triumphantly traverses the treble and the bottom.
All of your forefathers fought & not even death could stop them.
Know, now, that you were born to FIGHT the power.
So, knuckle up!
Tighten your laces, &
FIGHT!
& make it funky!

Darius, Can You Write Me A Poem?

You do not want
poetry.

You want quotables and
broad strokes.

You do not want
poetry's scalpel.

That first cut would feel
too much like Truth;

too much like mirrors in the morning.

You just want words to dance for you.
You want them to pirouette between lines,
stay in their place
between the margins.

You do not desire the reflection, the reveal.
You don't want the ugly.

There is plenty ugly in a poet's pen.
Sometimes a poet's breath is of bile;
it reeks of vile honesty.

Honestly, you just want the *still I rise*.
You don't want *history's shame* and *twisted lies*.

You don't want poetry.
You just want a poet to write you a smile.

But these things:
are the stone and chisel.
They are the clay,
the kiln and the forgotten creation
collecting dust in the corner.

These poems:
nesting
nightmares unearthed;
hopes desperate to
write themselves into existence.

Tool and creation.
Sin and salvation.
Earth and atmosphere.
The dirt. The dirty. The filthy.
The baptism of water and fire.

These poems are the cry and the embrace.

Being

Have you ever swallowed your entire *being*?
It is as hard as it sounds.
It feels like a heart attack in your throat
that hits, then sits in your chest.
Your *being*
sits in the middle of your chest,
grips your heart that beats too loud.
They tussle -
your heart and your swallowed *being*.
The tussle makes your chest heave uncontrollably.

I swallowed my *being* three times that night.

One –
blue and red lights.
Two in the morning.
Florida highway.
Campus-bound.
Ron, riding shotgun, fighting sleep for my sake.
Girls knocked out in backseat.
Those familiar lights brought my *being* out of me;
rested him on my tongue
so that he could see hands at 10 and 2
as we came to stop on the embankment.
My *being* began its crawl as I began to recall
"The Black Man Traffic Stop Rules."
It hit my stomach somewhere around
no sudden moves.

Two –
Step out of the car.
Am I going to jail?
I'm not made for jail.
I saw *Shawshank*.
And *Penitentiary*.
I made it all this way.
Mama's going to be "used-to-be" proud of me.
I'll be just like my uncles,
my cousins,
next door and 'round the corner neighbors.
The light beckoned my *being*;
it jumped to the back of my tongue to hide -
searching for darkness until incandescence
pushed it down my throat.
I opened the door and my *being*
danced in my belly as
fingers danced around
a holster.

Three –
a car backfires.
It was less of a swallow.
My *being* winning the tussle
until my heart froze like the rest of me.
Guns already been drawn.
Slurs already been hurled.
Threats already spit-painted on my face.
My *being* squeezed.
All I could hear was my Aunt Cynt singing,
Mama wailing in tongues,
Sister just asking me to wake up.

I could hear Granddaddy slipping in hellfire warnings between tales of my athletic failings and academic accolades.

Then,
    drive slow, ya hear?

 My *being* releases my heart.

I hear laughter -
in chorus.

Someone hands me paper as
boots march away.

My *being* spent the next two hours hiding.
I found it beneath my bed
holding my 5-year-old self,
singing, *"Every little thing is gonna be alright."*

Hand Over Heart

I'm gonna stand for the pledge
one day
when I can stand on the street
and not
be lynched for my full lips.
It's hard to say the pledge with full lips
or to stand with knees in my back
or to put my hand over my heart
when my hands are chained to poplar trees,
to bullshit and *Birth of a Nation*.
Liberty and justice still get stuck in barrels,
behind bullets buried in black bodies.

I'm going to stand proudly for the pledge.
I'll hold my hand over my heart,
I'll put my beer down and bellow the anthem
when my naps are no longer felonies,
when traffic stops are routine not roulette,
when my wallet is no threat to leave
my body bankrupt.
When "stop resisting" is no longer a greeting.

I stopped saying the pledge in the seventh grade.
I'd halfway read some Malcolm:
a weathered copy of *Autobiography* on
my local library shelf led me to believe
my protest was righteous.
Got sent to the principal.
Compromised revolution by standing,
lip-synching allegiance.
No more a class disruptor.
Disruption never killed anyone.
Okay, it has killed plenty.
But liberty and justice has always come with casualties.

That Time I Met Malcolm

He looked a lot like the loud-mouthed soldier from *Glory*.
That one-teared soldier from *Glory*.
He looked a lot like Bleek from *Mo' Bette*r.

He told me some things that made me more,
better.
He held up a mirror and in it I saw beautiful.

I saw my black as beautiful.
I saw my skin, not as sin, but salvation.
Me as messianic melanin.
I saw my intelligence as gorgeous.
I saw my vocabulary as vixen, as vivacious.
My ME as dangerous.

Do you remember that time I met Malcolm X?
Other people were there.
Uncle Skip was there.
Cuzzo was there.
Strangers were there,
but we, Malcolm and me, had our own conversation.

We talked about loving self
and knowledge as wealth.
We talked about things my mind was too young
to completely understand.
But I sat and listened like a good child.
Kernels being buried in my teeth and mind.

We didn't talk about Jesus, or Allah, or right or wrong.
He told me about cross burnings.
I told him about "we're closed signs"
and "niggers" hurled like rocks towards my young frame.

I met Malcolm again in the library.
I met him when I was learning how to fit into my black skin.
Those stories he told me the first time began to make sense.
This was more conversation than sermon.
He crawled from the pages and sat next to me.
He walked with me and sat with me at bus stops and benches.
He listened and whispered as my pen began to scribble
young boy dribble now draped and dripping in Kemetic jewels.

You met Malcolm yet?

He beautiful.

Butterfly

She is a butterfly:
beautifully blooming brilliance.
Resilience is her middle name.
She came through the muck and mire, blood and fire -
once had to crawl through her consequences,
now, she's ascending higher.

We should all aspire to be as she.

See, as she spreads her wings,
each flap brings her closer to the realization of her dreams,
the materialization of her desires.
No fly or bee could be as she.
Butterfly.
Bouncing from petal to bloom
blessing each place she lands,
bringing life just as she is born again.
A phoenix risen,
a soul engulfed in a prism of colors.
A painted lady.
Pain-tinted lady
that refuses to be contained by her surroundings.
Constrained by the sky, not she.
She is free.
And she was born to fly.

Black Boys Fly

Boy, you fly.
Boy, you so damn fly.
Boy, you so damn fly; look at your hair.
Look how your hair look like the clouds.
That's how fly you are.
Boy, you so damn fly they mistake you for birds.
You so damn fly you got that quail and condor effect.
Boy, you so damn fly they confuse you with birds.
They think you a bird.
You look like eagle or hawk the way you spread your wings.
Boy, you fly when you spread your wings.
You so damn fly they try to shoot you down.
They try to shoot you down out the sky
every chance they get.
But you better keep flying.
And you can
        fly, that is, 'cause you
Dr. J. + Jordan from the free throw fly.
Your soul shifts oxygen and redesigns sky.
Tropical storms form each time you cry.

Boy, you
Boy, you
Boy, you fly!

Lil' Man

Lil' Man caught fire 'round the corner from his house.
Somebody had to see it, but the street's a tight-clenched mouth -
except for screaming sirens
and the weeping from his mother.
And the promise of revenge from his cousins and his brother.
    "Cuz somebody gotta pay,"
but no one paid attention
to years of failing grades,
all the school days he was missing.
Never had a pot to piss in, so his aim remained distorted.
And all his childhood dreams had long ago been aborted.

Just a year ago you'd find him catching passes, breaking tackles,
now his flesh just caught the bullets -
bones breaking from the shrapnel.
He knew not of tassel or a graduation gown,
but he knew the daily hassle of moving bricks
and pushing pounds
and keeping head upon a swivel,
but he wasn't' fast enough
to escape all of his demons when the guns began to bust.

Thus, Lil' Man caught fire 'round the corner from his house.

Someone took his money, his work, his jewelry and his shoes.
Someone took his name, so they won't say it on the news.
Black Male is what they'll call him,
and they'll say that he was killed.
One small drop in the pool of all the blood that has been spilled.

And the street lights have retired, but police lights get overtime -
cashing checks and breaking necks
under the guise of stopping crime.

Cops are trading stories of the latest Netflix show
and taking bets on warrants of the regulars they know.

The corner store is buzzing just like nothing even happened.
Statues smoke on Newports and pretend that they ain't trapping.

Cars run by telling stories that reflect Lil' Man's demise.
While no one took the moment to go and close his eyes.
So, his eyes just see the concrete and the shoes off in the distance.
His cold lips kiss the spot that the homeless dog just pissed in.

Yes, Lil' Man caught fire 'round the corner from his house.

The school bus he once rode just let some students off.
They see the latest in the line of all the classmates lost.
They don't break their stride, just glance in his direction,
shake their heads and put their headphones in
for the next musical selection.

Even though Lil' Man caught fire
'round the corner from his house,
no one will be sleeping in his bed tonight
But his spot on the block will be quickly filled.
Applications and resumes already coming in
'cause one life don't stop the bills.

It'll be Ray Ray or J-Rock or some other nickname ready
to risk their lives for trinkets, 23s on their box Chevy.

And RIP t-shirts soon will flood the corners.
A cottage industry created from for all the mourning for the goners
like Lil' Man, who caught fire 'round the corner from his house.

And it happened just down the street from
Mt. Missionary Pentecostal.
And preacherman drives by with the compassion of
Hell's unholiest apostles.
Locked doors and rolled up windows on his darkly-tinted Benz.
On his way to meet the deacon's wife for some laying on of hands.

While Lil' Man's hands are cold now, and his lips are shaded blue.
Long way from kindergarten crayons and field trips to the zoo.
He and his kind are branded animals and
slaughtered like some prize,
But this baby kisses concrete and
no one has to yet to close his eyes…

Cuz Lil' Man caught fire 'round the corner from his house
Someone had to see it but the street's a tight-clinched mouth.

Poetry is a One Hour Forty-Three Minute Playlist

The Message

    is simply

I Ain't No Joke

    and neither are you.

I Know You Got Soul

    so, you better

Fight The Power

    cuz in this walk

Ain't No Half Steppin

    and

Dear Mama

    in the midst of it all, please

Keep Ya Head Up

    until eternity. Know that

The World Is Yours

    and though I may not deserve it

I Need Love

    Sometimes, it's my

Mind Playing Tricks on Me

    convincing me that

I Used to Love H.E.R.

    - you, and I only need

Me, Myself, and I

    and that

I Got It Made

    because being

Paid in Full

    is enough. Though I

Can't Knock The Hustle

    there is much more needed for true

Liberation

    Scream with me,

You Must Learn

    everything you can to

Bring the Pain

    to all corrupt systems that use our

Complexion

    gender, ethnicity, orientation, religion or class to

Regulate

    our existence. And let us create a

Slum Beautiful.

Soul Brotha

Aye, you got that new James Brown record?
That's a bad man.
A super bad man!

Who else move like dat?
Spin, groove like dat?
Change yo mood on the dime he spins on like dat?

That cat don't play no games.
James don't play tha radio.
He don't play on that radio.

He and Maceo
got you waking up
in cold sweats,
then pumping bold fists.

That's a bad man.
That's a black man.

You seen him on Ed Sullivan?
How he move like that?
He move like black gold electrified
He move like the Holy Ghost married a jook joint and
honeymooned on hot coals.

He hot. Cold. Pants. Sweat.

He make everybody forget.
He make everybody remember.

Like old pictures.
Like granddaddy stories.

He make everybody forget we black and they treat us like that.
He make everybody remember that we black and they treat us like that but we still got soul power.

How da music make you feel like Sunday dinner?
Like mac and cheese in yo knees.
Like potato pies in yo thighs.
Like yo feet frying in the same pan that got that chicken poppin'.

Stoppin' can't happen when that cat rappin'.
He be rappin'.
He be rappin' til you feel it.
He be rappin' to yo spirit.
He be rappin' like his life depend on it.
Like yo life depend on it.
He be rappin' for us.

You seen him on Ed Sullivan?
You seen them white people clapping?

Acting like they don't care that he black.
Like they don't care that he talk like that,
that he look like that.
Like they ain't scared of him and ain't scared of us.
Like that groove make everything equal.
Like he can't rally the people.
Like he can't take the power in his feet and put it in our fists.
Like he can't take the fight in his songs and put it in our tongues.

Why they acting like that?

Like he ain't saying it loud.
Like we ain't saying it loud.
Like he don't have soul power:
lightening in his feet,
thunder clapping in his voice.
Can't they see, they hear that he us?

Aye, you got that new James Brown record?

You betta.
It's like being baptized in baselines and Black Panther.

Yo soul might just get saved.

Eric B. for President of the Deacon Board

Songs by Eric B. & Rakim were my hymns.
Holy ghost; I ain't no joke.
The god was him.
Gold ropes.
Medallion.
Messiah's hair like wool traded for box fade.
Salvation paid in full on stage -
behind mic.
Eric B. on the cut
creating masterful mosaics made to accompany poetry like
the organist in the back of the Baptist church
painting over the pastor's parables -
soft or loud - his sermons move the crowd.

Yooos replace amens
as Rakim preached;
hands in the air signaled hallelujah to the technique.

I let my tape rock until I could recite his songs like scripture.
I knew *Paid in Full* better
than any epistle Paul lettered.
The 18th Letter:
righteous redemption in rhymes.
In my mind, rap rescinded the rapture;
captured the ear of this confused, conflicted kid,
kept him eager to listen.
Album playing in head
kept him constant sermon-missing,
wishing the deacon would stop singing

> *Wade in the water.*
> *Wade in the water, children.*

And just press play and
let the rhythm hit 'em.
Baptism by lyrical wizardry.
Preach, brother, Preach.
Teach the children.

Sip the juice like communion wine.

Knowing the ledge made 23rd Psalm seem to salute
the god of rhymes,
Shakespeare of his time.

>[1]Rakim is my shepherd and I am like his sheep.
>[2]He makes me nod my head as I try to *keep the beat*;
>   he leads me to dictionaries to define words he used,
>[3]He restores an unknown love for jazz and the blues;
>   he leads an entire generation with his lyrical syncopation,
>   weaving webs with words to capture imaginations.
>[4]Yea, though I bop through school hallways in the Sunshine State,
>   I felt like I was on a stoop in Queens, boombox and crates:
>   for the 'R' is with me, hit me with lyrics and melody,
>   Eric B. killing with cuts so much it should be a felony.
>[5]You set the table for those you inspired to use complex lyricism
>   and set the mic afire;
>   you anointed future MCs, passed the torch and inspired
>   Those with soul and skill to attack it;
>[6]Surely goodness followed as you begat *Illmatic* and more:
>   as we sift through the subpar and metaphors that keep missing,
>   I will forever remain *eager to listen*.

Feel Jesus

You make me feel Jesus.
Your skin - garment hems.
Your skin is a garment I want to crawl into,
break in until it don't feel new no more.
It don't smell new no more,
like 2nd semester sophomore year of college everyday jeans.
Like the used-to-be black tee that helps hide my flaws.
Like shoes with the right amount of bend above my toes,
the perfect bit of give in my soul.
There is salvation in your touch,
Lazarus in the linger of your fingertip.

You make me feel Moses.
Your lips are red seas.
Sometimes pink seas
Sometimes seas so natural I dive in, float in – fearless.
The part when they first part stays on repeat in my mind.
On rewind is you saying the words *pepper* and *beautiful*.
You have burning bush on your tongue.
Ten commandments outline your teeth like open face golds.
There is salvation in your speak.
Holy ghost in your *hello*.
Your kiss kills Pharaoh in me.
Your kiss builds the pharaoh in me.

Sometimes you make me feel like Daniel.
Or Shadrach.
Or Meshac.
Abednego.

Sometimes you are a lion in a furnace.
Roaring flames singeing places I thought were sacred.
Bite this; burn this heart of mine
and I just call on God.
The same God that sewed your garment and painted your seas
has given you the gift of melting my face,
clenching your teeth around my faith until I can't walk away.

I am Saul turned Paul.
I am convert.
There are mustard seeds in my pupils.
I see heaven where you see flaw.

I *Hallelujah* at the sight of you, holy sacrament.

You are communion.
The body and the blood.
I am baptized by your beautiful.

Amen

Marvin's Mystique

Father, Father…
I request a conversation that one might expect to be one-sided,
but you speak to me.
Even after the day the earth and sun collided -
divided the heavens from here where the mere mortals abide.
And I, like a Greek farmer lamenting to father Zeus
for a bountiful harvest.
To you, father Marvin, and for you, I've cried.
Eyes pouring over like wells,
Like yours for Ms. Terrell.

And you speak to me as if you've casted spells
on 8-tracks and vinyls.
Inspired minds to break backs, shift spinal cords
to chords that were Funk Brother concocted and crafted:
syncopation with angel wings and church mother moans,
gifted, guttural, emboldened tones.
Your golden songs adorned ears, allayed fears and have served as
symphonic serenades played as background music for countless
bouts of love made.

How many black babies have you to thank for their existence?
Resistance was never an option once your concoction of
confidence and vulnerability
mixed with unbridled virility dripped,
slipped into the ears of the good girl
fighting to keep her panties around her waist.
You made sin saintly.

You helped paint me poet.
Placed pen in my hand.

I feel your falsetto in my fingertips.
On lips are questions and answers,
the rhythm of dancers, a soldier's tenacity,
and a grandmother's grace.

I fight to keep pace.
Since that shot from your Pops caused your heart to stop,
mine has been racing,
chasing after you who sings songs in keys Stevie never could play.
Chasing after you like you would chase the highs,
but catch the lows way too often,
hoping "she" would soften the blow.
But all the "shes" never filled the voids of that young boy that
continued to cry out 'What's going on?"

So, tell me: what is going on?

Have you met God?
What is She like?
Did She select you to direct the heavenly choir,
or are you headlining, sequined jacket shining at
Club Fire and Brimstone?

Since you've been gone,
did you know that you have become synonymous with the words
soul,
icon,
legend?
Do you laugh when you hear sycophant singers
seeking to ascend to your sanctity
and claim you as inspiration?

Do you hear them fail…fall…like notes on strained chords?
Voices forcing what you expressed as easy as exhales.
Do you smile?
Or does it make you you wanna holla (the way they do your life?)

Your life…

How do you view your life, your choices?
Like lovelorn lovers and loveless loved ones lamenting over lost
or self-righteous renegades reveling in decisions made no matter
the cost?

I hope the latter,
for the former would shatter all that I have built you to be:
this Eifel Tower of power crafted in complexity,
a pyramid built with blocks of *I love yous* and *fuck yous*
simultaneously.
The genius antithesis of what they claimed sane to be.

Oh, how you sang to me.

I, young and fragile,
not yet knowing what I did not know.

But I knew I found solace at your altar.
You played the part of preacher gladly.

Your psalms like
calming balms for the mad me,
comfort for the sad me,
reassurance for the sometimes egotistical and occasionally
devilishly bad me.

Strong, but silvery tones.
Baritones tickled marrow bones shook all the way home
from the backseat of Mama's Pontiac Bonneville Brougham.
You definitely had me:
Musically and lyrically begat me.
My mother's intellect and strong will mixed with your soul,
tortured and beautiful to behold,
singing away the oft sad me.
It was like you sat me right next to you and proceeded
to give me everything I needed:
a litany of symphonies about life's opera
occasionally stopping the lesson to pontificate
about masochism or religion
or masochism as a religion.
Gems hidden in hymns found on vinyl and cassette
became hard to forget.
Words circling your rhythm became my catechism.

Who pays the price? The artist.

Blood, sweat, soul gets pulled in a multitude of directions.
Not just cathartic,
but sacrificing self to help the broken-hearted,
the close-minded.
For those that seek peace,
the answer
or the question,
you help find it.

Often blinded and deafened by the world's intention
to lessen a connection to source,
I talk to you and get realigned -
course redefined.

Finding solace in my soul's soldering of the sacred and secular.

For I know we have no time to wait...
got to pray and meditate.
And that it's okay to say I can't wait for you to operate.

Thank you.
For you sharing soul.
For being painfully open and vulnerable

and allowing us to be witnesses to genius incarnate

in our lifetime.

For the Sun When Clouds Block Her Shine

Hearts cannot break.
They can be stretched
      bruised
           pulled
           sullied
      neglected,
but they cannot be broken.
Woven into the tendrils of the heart
is god stuff.
      Your very heart beats miracle -
      left and right ventricles echo overcoming.
Summon your goddess.
      Even when you've allowed them
      to smudge your crown,
you are still queen.
Royalty knows pain,
      heartstrings may become frayed
      but are gold and moonlight-crafted, so
hearts can't break.
They are eternal.
You are eternal.

Lying Feels Like Dying But Costs Less Than Caskets

Some day in the distant (or not-so-distant future,)
I may find myself draped in scrubs,
sweaty brow and sweaty palms offering rubs
to the shoulders, back, and belly
of the mother of my soon-to-be born.
I will offer all the moral support I can muster,
allow her to squeeze my hand,
nails sink in, break skin, but I will stand.
I'll stand as her suddenly sailor-like tongue
delivers a tirade that should make me question her parenting skills.
Until
        that moment
                      that beautiful moment of birth.

And we'll smile.
And we'll cry and the only thought in my mind would be
all the lies and half-truths I'm going to have to tell my seed.
Like,
    Baby,

        I promise that Mommy and Daddy will always be together;
        there will never be anything stronger than this family.
        Family never fails.

        And there are no monsters under your bed,
        and those outside your window can never get in;
        you are invincible.

        And you can be anything you want in this world.

    My son,
        the world is not as scary as you may think.
        It's okay to cry.
        You can succeed if you try.

Your melanin is not a sin;
and though you must always be aware and
lights will one day shine in your face for no reason;
your face may kiss the concrete for no reason;
It may seem like open season on people that look like you,
you will make it.
Like I did.
but better than me.

Because you'll have both mommy
and daddy, guaranteed.
You won't have to fight your way
from porch to the end of the street.
You won't have to sit on the couch
staring out the window waiting for me.

Baby girl,
    you are not seen as lesser than.
    your gender is not a scarlet letter.
    they will respect your divinity.
    you don't have to be afraid.
    walking alone does not make you more prone to violence.
    no one expects your silence.
    what you wear does not make you a target.
    men are inherently good.

You see, I would make a good father
despite the lack of a role model.
My son would never have to curse me,
spit in my face for dropping him
twenty birthday dollars three weeks late.

My daughter will never have to go through life
blindly trying to find the love of a man only to find
devils desiring to devour her divinity
and diminishing her self-worth,
because daddy will be there and
she'll know diamonds don't compare to her smile.

And standing in that delivery room,
staring into the eyes of my daughter/son
I know I'll have to tell them that
> *I am a superhero.*
> *And that bullets can bounce off my back.*
> *And I am faster than the speed of sound and can*
> *corral racist rants before they reach my baby's ears.*
> *And I am stronger than the weight of oppression*
> *pressing down on us.*

I cannot tell them that their daddy is but a fragile man.
A man that has been broken, heart and spirit.
I cannot tell them that fear constantly creeps 'cross and
cradles in the crevices of my consciousness.
I cannot tell them that life is harder than you think.
I cannot tell them that my love, as strong as it is, does not ensure
them safety.
And that the holes in my hands are from bullets when I asked them
not to shoot.

I am no Christ.
I may not be able to save them.
I can only lie to them and pray.
and hope I am half the father featured in all the lies I'll say.

It Just Makes Cents

The danger must be the plastic
They were worried about the carbon footprint
Those tiny parcels must be met with force
The law's fullest extent meant to preserve the planet
    Damn it, Unc.
Had you just sold your weed in glass bottles
or as gummies
in dispensaries with ambient lighting and health
plans for your employees,
you might still be able to vote.

ride the jam pony express or how to get dope boys to dance down South

Once upon a time a lemon met a lime
Had sex one night and made a baby named Sprite
                              - Jam Pony Express DJs

Hip Hop started out in the parks,
in the boroughs -
The Bronx ,
The Boogie Down.
Bounced to Brooklyn and beyond,
but what about a black boy in the Bottom?
Broward.
By birth, Bass became my baseline.
Trunks rattled, sounds splattered
and booty shorts were all the rage.
Dade kept us bouncing.
The crews were 2 live and the
DJs felt like your uncle at the family reunion:
in tune with the streets and the culture.

South Florida – more than just salsa and hurricanes.

You don't think music made its way below the Mason-Dixon?
We, too, let our tapes rock until they popped.
Scotch helped save the day on many occasion
when radio stations wouldn't do.

We, too bumped Beat Street and back-spinned
on refrigerator boxes.

Up rocked and pop-locked and knew all the
scenes in *The Last Dragon*.

Am I the baddest mofo low down around this town?

But you had to get the music.
And you had to get it infused with
funk the Florida way.

You had to get the real.
And none realer than
Jam Pony Express DJs
delivering dimes that caused constant replays and
"what did he say?" right before tapping rewind.
Then, we'd find a new verbal gem by
Him.
Them.
They.

Maestros.
Flawlessly fading like some funk-filled phantasm finessing
New York's finest flows with some South Florida flavor.

"Ouu, Lawd."
        Like a religious experience while Eric Sermon warned
        us of the danger zone.

Any time a new Jam Pony tape dropped,
we Flea Market copped then copied it,
so we could rock it
and sing along like
campfire songs on broken city streets.

Gritty beats slow-motioned around corners.
Donk trunks rattled up and down the block.

LL was bad, but became badder with
Slick Vic, Big Ace and Lock Cool Jock urging all to

    Ride out, now.

More commandment than suggestion.
City boy's sliding with figure skate grace.

    Ride out, now.

        Slide
        Slide
        Slide
        Slide.

Corner Store Sonnets

One

They stand and smoke Newports, Camels, or Kools;
take sips of aluminum in brown bags.
We pass them as we trudge our way to school.
Cautionary tales against skipping class.

They were once us; precocious and chasing
dreams we still believe are within our reach.
Lustfully, running behind girls; facing
trouble for not letting their teachers teach.

What is it – that oft-glazed stare in their eyes?
What part disappointment? What part regret?
Do they look on us with love; do they despise
our chance to get the things they did not get?

They sip, trading tales of achievements past,
blowing smoke, like their hope, that could not last.

Next

Y'all remember when they shot Mr. James?
He was griot. Sage. Shaman. Scholar.
The whole just block stopped; a got damn shame.
What he had on him? A chain? Twelve dollars?

You'd find him posted, wall-leaning daily.
Magic cigarette bottom-lip dangling.
Dropping gems, jewels; sometimes quotes crazy
like Ozzie's Da Mayor - *Do The Right Thing*.

Yo. Why they get him? Them niggas ain't shoot
them boys Steve or Money or Los, them cops,
any terror that has shackled, put boots
on necks, stomped through, pissed on and killed or crops.

Shootin' easy when they ain't shooting back.
Guess it's always easy when shooting black.

Third

Some days the corner store seemed much too far
a walk to make before the late bell rang.
We'd take a short cut - racing past parked cars,
hands on pockets, hoping to not drop our change.

Change we'd rescued from a cushiony jail -
free from dirty popcorn, hairballs, and lint,
now fuzzy, sticky barter for the sale.
Unearned money was never better spent.

Ms. Jones pulls back the screen door, smiles and quips,
"Baby, what you want? Don't you take all day."
Nown Laters, *picka leg*, barbecue chips,
and a freeze cup. You got pink lemonade?

Now, we sit in class on a fructose high.
Failing to figure the square root of pi.

Everywhere Ain't For Everyone

While riding
across the United States
on a train, my friend
sent pictures
from her cabin window:
trees
rumbling rivers
rustic railroads
lakes – trembling and tranquil
Magnolias (I think)
a house nestled in
Virginian hills surrounded by
more trees: pines, cypress,
maybe sycamores.

The house:
idyllic
beautiful
palatial
split-level
balconies
most certainly an Olympic-sized
pool.

My first thought:
      "Damn, that looks like the house from *Get Out*."
Second thought:
      "I hope she lives."

That Daisy in the Dirt is Us
A Golden Shovel

Shout out to Queen Gwendolyn Brooks
Shout out to Terrance Hayes

She often complained about the time we
would spend, or the lack thereof. She felt love was real
only when present. Only when cool
nights were comforted with warm hugs. We
rarely had those nights. Our work or play left
us clinging to phone calls and messages. Unc tried to school
me when I was a youngin'. Said balls made us different. Meant we
need to hang and breathe. We weren't made to lurk
and linger. Fingers trace and legs race to late
night calls. Boy, men were made to fly. And I thought we -
she and I - had that understanding, but to strike
a match does not ensure the flame. Straight
away, wind came and blew out the fire. We
tired of love songs. Hellish choirs would now sing
our sin.
Our wrongs written on the back of eye lids when we
dreamt of others. That thin
girl at the store, the gin
and juice friend from your college days. We
pretended not to know. Improvising like Jazz
riffs, but the riffs began to shine like Florida June
at noon. Heat became unbearable; we
didn't plan on our love's burial, but I guess everything must die.
Just didn't know it would be this soon.

BSL Blues

Sung in the style of any classic Blues Man or Kool Moe Dee record

Playing football -
your boy's too fast.
Two-hand touch in the street.
Tackle in the grass.

Touchdowns: the white Caddy
and the green garbage can.
If the Caddy move,
it's Ms. Johnson's Brown van. (The van never, ever moves.)

Third game this week.
We haven't won yet.
Sean always talking junk.
We made a two-dollar bet.

We got ball first;
drew plays in the sand.
Sean guarding me.
I'mma kill this man.

Marc's cousin, Dre,
was all-time quarterback.
So, there'd be no rushing.
There would be no sacks.

Down, set…
But before he said *hike*.
Someone yelled *hey*
and pointed at the street lights.

I saw the flicker.
And my heart skipped a beat.
Snatched my ball;
raced down the street.

The game was over
before it begun.
We lost track of time,
betrayed by the Sun.

My hand hit the doorknob
before the lights shone.
Mama sat on the couch.
Family Matters was on.

I watched Steve Urkel
with a half-hearted grin.
I missed an ass-whooping
but lost a chance to win.

Brown boys all over
have been in my shoes.
We can all sing in chorus
the *Before Street Light Blues*.

Atlanta Pirates

Back when ripping cellophane CD wrappers was a thing,
my red Ford Escort was our small crew's boombox on wheels.
I drove: M in the front, T in the back but elbows
impatiently resting on console for the unveiling.
The court for sport our destination;
no clue what the journey ahead would bring.
My hands - no where near 10 and 2, seat angled obtuse.
Pine fresh dangling from rearview.
Change and folded dollars for gas in cup holder.
I, designated driver. M, our future fumbling in his hands.
T, mumbling about last night's shenanigans.
'Pac and The Roots bounce back and forth, but only in
anticipation of M's hands -
slow like his dribble,
ineffective like his crossover.
Red light.
I snatched.
      "Gimme that."
Slid CD in slow before the light turned green.

    Lord, it's so hard living this life of constant struggle each and every day.

Five by nines turned up too loud
whistled out Baptist hymns dripped in
ghetto realism.
Real nigga quotes wrapped in Southern drawl.
That *Soul Food* fed us like Grandma's Sunday
dinner on a Saturday afternoon.

    What y'all niggas know about the Dirty South?

Slang twang.
If booty shake and Rakim had a baby,
maybe it would sound like that last verse on *Goodie Bag*.
Had us holding our heads like, "yo, man! You heard what he said?"

> *No, I don't carry an ax, but I still swing low with the lumberjacks.*

Before long, hatchback parked at the court with
doors flung,
trunk popped.
Ball stopped.
Sweat dripped as heads nodded
to this noise organized in Atlanta dungeon
sounding like a collective experience;
sounding impoverished and articulate.
Faces twisting,
necks flexing,
heads bouncing 'cause

> *They put us to the test – women and men; if you black, you in.*

We knew something 'bout the Dirty South.
We knew fenced in and marginalized.
We knew ghetto birds and pushing birds and
bird-chested boys battling on streets they would never own,
running to get home before the street lights shone fear on
their dark sin.

> *Everything that I did, different things I was told*
> *just ended up being food for my soul.*

That became Summer's soundtrack:
parks,

block parties,
driveway pontification.
Other joints found their way on, but we found our way back
to 808s, hums, and a high-pitched poetic preacher with pinpoint
parables.
Radicals that sounded like country cousins rapping
between spades at the family reunion.

Uncles exhorting - *use that tool between your two shoulders* while regaling
in stories of how shorty look(ed) good wit' them hairy legs.

We were fed.

what do ghosts smell like?

I remember when I first realized my uncle was not my uncle.
He had been renamed.
> *Addict.*
> *Fiend.*
> *Smoker.*
> *Crackhead.*
> *Baser.*

Grandma was choking on her tears; crying on her Jesus pages.
She hadn't seen/ heard from him in days.
Hadn't seen him or the 50 dollars
for a used lawnmower so he could cut a few yards.
She worried between parables and cried hard.
I, adolescent innocent and hardly hardened, worried with her.
Wondered if he had been shot/got by some bad guy.
I cried with Grandma that night.
Imagined the worst - holding her hand in funeral procession,
wiping weeping from her face,
trying not to leave traces of Kleenex.
I've always been Grandma's Buddha.

The smell of crack is distinct.
It stinks like burning sulfur and melted tomorrows.
Crack houses smell worse -
littered with glass pipes, aluminum cans
and Langston Hughes dreams crusting in the corners of mouths
We - me, Grandma, Jesus - stumbled through.
Stepping over huddled masses and broken hopes,
fighting through smoke thickness only interrupted by sparks from lighters

We found him on his way down.

Dazing.
Gazing and glassy.
Pupils dilated, whole eye painted a poverty yellow.
Grandma pleaded with the blood of Jesus and praying oil,
but he refused,
angrily spewed cuss words my young ears had heard,
but not with such conviction.
And not in earshot of her.
Disbelief drips then springs from her lips.
    Kevin? Kevin?! Kevin!!! That ain't nothing but the devil!
My tiny hands trying to pull her away.
Wanting to save her and pummel him at the same time.
That was not my uncle, but a ghoul; a ghost.
We left,
but that ghost would visit often.
Sometimes wearing Uncle Kevin's charisma.
Other times fully exposed.
It would take with it TVs and trust
and leave behind tears of guilt and dusty shelves.

I would try to help Grandma see the ghost,
but she only saw her son,
only saw her failings

Years later, I reminded him of that night.
Of all the nights and days,
the missing money from piggy banks,
the barefooted and filthy appearances
after months away.
I asked him
the why
the what
the how.

And he was honest and calm,
And, for a moment, he was my uncle.

But his eyes turned glassy between blinks.
Every so often he had to brush away crusted over dreams.

And today, I know my uncle as ghost.
Afraid of the darkness.
Unable to live, but dying with no success.

That ghost – still knocking, still haunting
my grandmother – still afraid to see the truth.

Jit

Urban Dictionary: another word for kid, youngsta.

Lil' jit bad.
Jit always 'round here talking.

Shut up, jit.
Hush up, jit, before I tell your mama.
You ain't nothing but a jit.

Damn, lil' jit got some heart.
Jit ain't scared to fight.

Hey, watch out for jit; he can shoot that rock.
Jit'll take it to the hole on you.

Y'all seen jit that used to be around here?
I heard jit done dropped outta school.
Last time I seen jit, he was slangin' over there off 27th.
Jit and 'nem wild.
Jit stay strapped and always talking reckless about what he'll do.
    Jit don't know who he is.
    Jit searching for self in all the wrong places.
    Jit was never equipped with the mechanisms to cope.
    Jit can't figure out proper channels for trauma.
    Jit could've used more positive role models.
    Jit could've used some counseling.
Y'all heard about jit?
Jit mama asking 'bout him.
Jit gone.
Jit ain't coming back.

At least, not that jit.
Jit name was Travis.
They ain't have to do jit/Travis like that.
Somebody should've talked to jit/Travis before it was too –

Hey, who this jit right here?
Jit bad.

Odes to Little Black Boys Before They Don't Get the Chance to Become Black Men

1.

Don't ever let anybody tell you that you ain't god!

But don't ever tell a black woman she ain't god!

You both be god.
See god in your lips that speak gospel and hip hop,
in her hips that tell stories everybody ain't ready to hear.

Be god.
See god in those waves – those waves you've been brushin' –
those waves bustin' like Atlantic tides
coming in on coasts sang about in anthems
and dirges.
See god in her passion – righteous anger is in her side-eye.
Pursed lips might prevent Armageddon.

Don't let nobody tell you that you ain't, y'all ain't god.

They don't know no better.
They've been fed false prophets.

Just drop some castor oil on their eyes
and watch the scales fall.

2.

Somewhere between brush cut and waves
and unkempt fro,
you might break a comb or two.
Your face will contort as black-fisted picks pull and stretch.

Naps pop as you bury your neck in your shoulders,
bracing for inevitable pain.

Get used to it.

They'll try to break, contort, pull, stretch, and pop you.
Protect your neck.
Your shoulders got gold between them.

3.

Ain't a damn thing wrong with your skin.
She just don't know how beautiful she is yet,
    Ain't no way she gone recognize your glow.

If you make it there,
    You gone be the shit on the other side.

Let it shine. Let it shine. Let it shine.

Milk On Her Mouth

I am sitting in a restaurant.
In the booth next to me, a precocious, doe-eyed daughter peeks
over purple vinyl peeling from years of stories rubbed against it.
She smiles – silly and snaggle-toothed.
    How many times must I tell you to sit down?
She is scolded, demanded, continuously reprimanded
when she stands up,
leans over and smiles at me.
The mother, barely a mother, gives a *sorry* to me that I shake off.
Baby's eyes start to well.
I want to hug them both,
tell them of their beauty and
how that smile dripped honey into my eyes,
    but I don't want to be a bother.
Don't want to overstep my bounds.
So, I sit and sip my tea – green -
wiping baby's tears in my mind.
I am no father, yet.
But if I get there, will I wear the skin of oppressor?
Don't move!
Don't laugh!
Don't speak!
Don't walk too fast, slow, out of line,
out of synch with how I think you should be!

As children, we need the chance to dance
when there seems to be no music,
for we still hear the private concerts god plays for us.

A child getting hands dirty, playing in mud, eating blades of grass
has recent recollections of being dust
and is just tasting her memories.

We trade drawing hopscotch squares and jumping rope
for needing hops, scotch, and squares just to cope.

We forget the joy we found in bubbles -
blowing bubbles,
blowing bubbles of spit,
blowing bubbles of snot.

Fascinated now only when bubbles pour out of bottles,
make us hobble to cars we can't afford -
a long way from Matchbox.

I contort my face when young mama ain't looking
just to let baby girl (and myself) know I still got some child in me.

When I was Tina and Grandma was Ike

There are few things worse than staring at a cold bowl of grits
with hot eggs and bacon on the table.
Scrambled, crispy and within reach,
but not for me.
Eat them grits, Grandma demanded.
Be grateful.
       They were hot and buttered.

But there I sat
in a stare down with
this bowl of grits
until they became cold and clumpy.
Until the table became barren but for the
stubborn boy with tears and snot dried on his face,
hands and arms and shoulders sore from Grandma's
pops and pinches,
stomach not understanding my decision to leave it
in discomfort.
There were hungry children somewhere who
would kill for these grits.
In my head, I sucked my teeth and wondered
why we couldn't
let *them* eat them,
pack them and send with Mama
on her mail route.

But I just sat -
Determined.
Resilient.
Hungry.
Crying.

I was not going to break;
I was not eating grits that day.
But Grandma had lived
through Jim Crow and childbirth.
She cared not for my weeping.
My first grandchild status did not provide me
cover that day.
Dinner came –
Grandma's expertly fried chicken.
Milky mashed potatoes and
golden corn.

I hadn't moved.
I ate grits –
clumpy, congealed,
mixed with mucus, tears and life lessons.

Sugar Water

Oil and water do not mix.
Neither do sugar and water,
but that didn't stop us
from scooping spoonfuls of diabetes
into cups of lead poisoning.
What else were we to do with no Kool-Aid
in the cabinet?
No fresh juice in the fridge?
Milk made stomachs hurt before
there was a name for it.
So, we stirred – fighting
to make our cups' content cloudy.
Oh, how'd we drink and think nothing.
Laughing at Scooby and Shaggy.
Pop Tarts and Hot Pockets on plates.
Sitting on floors, because
the TV was in the room with Grandma's good couches.

We were our own private Jesuses -
transforming water into tomorrow's addictions.
Insulin in our future but we felt
He-Man hyped.
By the power of Sucrose!!!
I'm jumping on this couch to drop
flying elbows on my cousin before
I entangle her in a figure-four leglock.

How often do we take purity
and taint it in the name of
pleasure or ignorance?

Like putting sugar into water,
we never think about the cavities
until there's a drill in our mouths.

There is an innocence in killing your future self
and laughing at that which is not real.

You should write more _____ stuff, they say

I sat down
to write a poem about love, but
it's hard to find pretty words
when you stay looking
over your shoulder
and around corners
and out your windows
and inside your house
and everywhere, cause anywhere
could be where my black gets me dead.

So, I stand up
to write about love, but
I do it slowly
and I write in my head
so my hands are visible
no pen
cuz blue bullets
beat black ink every time.

The pen's might is only in
signatures on amendments
and bills
and warrants
and death certificates.

So, I lie down
to write about love,
facedown,
arms and legs spread.
I try to write about love
But I wonder if I
Should draft my own
Eulogy instead.

Dae'kwon

Dae'kwon is eleven.
Dae'kwon is all knee scrapes and spit bubbles.
Dae'kwon is a good boy. He's straight A's and pleases and thank yous.
Dae'kwon is growth spurts and math tests and Sunday school naps,
but yes,
he can recite the 23rd Psalm.
Dae'kwon is calm.
                    Often.
Dae'kwon tries to be rough but softens up when Grandma calls.
He's Grandma's baby.
Dae'kwon is adolescent lazy.
Dae'kwon is video-game controller controlling and sore losing.
He is "boy, I ain't gone tell you again to take out that trash."

Dae'kwon is sloppy yet somewhat effective crossover
and all jump in his jump shot.
Dae'kwon is eight push-ups then flop.

Dae'kwon is "that's my girlfriend," which means he gives her his
cookie at lunch.

Dae'kwon is a good boy. He's straight A's and pleases and thank yous.

Dae'kwon is black.
He real black. He black like me.
He "can't be confused with anything but black" black.
I see myself in him.

I was Dae'kwon.
Name similar and handcuffed at five for not knowing I needed to run.

Dae'kwon is all run. All race. All sun, sweat on his face.
All love. All listen.
When I speak, he listens.

So, how do I tell Dae'kwon that he has been born into a skin that
attracts Taser beams, baton blows, and bullets?

How do I tell him that before he feels hair on his upper lip
he's liable to feel cuffs upon his wrists?

I don't have any children, but I always wondered how I would breathe
the news of no Santa to them.
How I would confess to being both St. Nick and the tooth fairy.
That I am not the world's strongest man or smartest man.

> *Confessions make innocence disappear, and harsh realities taste a lot like fear.*
> *Scary truths never want to be confronted.*

Dae'kwon is a good boy, and he listens to me.

I have instilled in him that hard work plus dedication equal success.
So, how do I admit to being a liar –
      having painted his brain with bright,
      vivid colors that don't exist for him?
Don't exist for names with arbitrary punctuation
or imaginative pronunciation.

How do I tell him that written on his forehead
and on their tongues is failure?
Is threat.
Is clenched purse and crossed sidewalks
Is prison numbers tabulated from test scores.

How do I explain that he has four brothers and
statistics fold sheets on prison beds waiting for two of them?

How do I tell him that he should never be ashamed of his name,
but that teachers will always find it hard to say,
but expertly quote the last name
of his classmates with Polish ancestors?

Those names sound like "right."

Dae'kwon sound like nigger.
Like frisked and searched.
Like clenched fists and stand your ground.

Dae'kwon sound like Medgar, like Emmett,
especially when it's said with a little Bull Connor in it.
Dae'kwon sounds eerily close to Tamir.
Exactly like ignorance-fueled fear.
Dae'kwon sounds hashtag-ready.

Dae'kwon is eleven.
Voice hasn't changed yet.
7 years from being able to vote;
7 seconds from being a threat.

Soon, Dae'kwon will realize his blackness.
Someone will purpose to make him feel less than.
Someone will treat him as more than Dae'kwon.
They will treat him like his name is danger.
Like his name is destruction.
Like his name is remedial, rape, robbery…
robbing the innocence before I can tell him that
Dae'kwon, even when said softly, could sound obituary.

Dae'kwon is eleven.
Dae'kwon is a good boy. He's straight A's and pleases and thank you.

Dae'kwon and I will talk…in front of the mirror.

I wonder if we will cry.

Black Girl Wonderful

Always under scrutiny and scorn.
Lovelorn,
torn limb from limb by a world that has deemed her worthless.
Constantly hurt, this girl consistently told that
"shake that, twerk this" is where her value dwells.
That your flesh sells and your spirit is but a burden.
For my nieces:
Princesses, I vow to see you grow into queens.
My heartbeats: left and right ventricles;
it is essential that you are kept strong.
Listen,
I know Grandma wants you in church, but take this poem.
Make it your bible.
For in this cruel world it will be essential for survival.

Chapter 1; Verse [1] in the **Book of Uncle D**:

You are worthy of high praise.
I've raised my hand to no woman except to bless
my calloused fingertips to caress her soft skin.
Accept nothing less.
Verse[2]:
Your worth is not measured by those still tethered
to society's archaic way of thinking.
Thinking is not an activity relegated to men,
so spend time in thought.
Get caught in whimsies of contemplation,
for you are brilliant.
For you are brilliant,
and your minds are what make the night starry.

Verse[3]:
I am sorry. I apologize for the empty facades and hopeless fantasies
to which you may fall prey.
Those homemade cards for your mommy on Father's Day.
All those times you've asked and will ask,
and he did not and will not stay.
Verse[4]:
Have nerve. Have pride.
Walk like you own the place, CEO in every stride.
Verse[5]:
I have never lied to you.
Words are super glue; convictions and reputation stick to you
like stickers stick on the back of car windows;
don't let yours fade, peel, or crack.
Verse[6]:
You're black. And a woman. And the sad fact
is that's like trying to play baseball with no arms,
but you better bite that bat.
Swing!
Because there are no excuses.
No reasons for failure.
The system is corrupt and it will definitely fail you,
but make sure you never ever fail yourself.
Verse[7]:
Your idea of romance may be tied to the lies
you hear through earbuds and speakers.
Venom-laced rhythms move feet, entice you to dance
but entrance you to think that courting is sporting.
Never play in a game if you can't help to set the rules.
Verse[8]:
Listen.
The universe yells in the rustle of leaves,
screams in those silent moments between question and response.

Give them time.
Verse[9]:
And, thus, trust your gut/intuition,
that little voice whispering and tickling the back of your neck.
She knows. She knows.

This is for all the little black girls forced to tightrope walk through this world.

Verse[10]:
Don't look down.
Your head should always be held high to account for your crown
and your eyes always fixated on the wonder to come.

Black girl
Black girl…beautiful
Black girl…wonderful
Black girl…marvelous
Black girl

The Undying of Tamir Rice

Y'all see Tamir?
He just got a fresh line up.
Outfit on point – freshly pressed.
Not too much starch.

Shoes crisp.
Snow white.
He's getting ready
for the first day of school.

This year,
he'll be consumed with biology
labs, essays, SATs, and
hormones.

School lunch will still
be suspect, but he'll
bond with friends, old and new,
debating albums, NBA stats, video
games and doing dumb teenage boy shit.

Tamir will probably
struggle a little in math class because
the girl he's had a crush on since
freshman year sits right in front of him.

He finds it hard to focus, thinks
making the basketball team might
help his chances.

He looks forward to the school dance
though he and his friends will probably
post up on a wall the whole night.

He'll get his license and the talk.
He'll hear the warnings, but he's a teenager.
All teenagers think they're superheroes.
But, he will eventually get pulled over
one day.

At least he'll be prepared this time.

I, Too, Am America and I'm Gone Sing/Aretha not Adele

after Langston Hughes

I, too, sing America.
      A song in keys broken
      Token harmonies imbedded in
      cacophonies
      My song is a scream
      Full-throated bellow
      Voice like sandpaper
      Dear neighbor
      face the music.

I am the darker brother.
      Darker sister
      Sun-kissed
      Different hue
      Different shade
      For far too long my
      song has been played
      on mute

They send me to eat in the kitchen
      but I have tended fields and
      seasoned pots and
      chopped, boiled, and fried -
      and fed their children, so

When company comes,
      I will sit
      napkin neatly folded
      holding fork and knife
      I will eat and

      I will drink
      I will speak of truths that
      turn stomachs and
      erase appetites
      Nice will not be on
      the menu. Dark
      stark realities will.
      They will feel
      They may cry

But I laugh,
      Full-throated laughs from my
      belly.
And eat well,
And grow strong.
      Because I know this
      is not new
      But I have no delusions of
      symphonies to be sung

Tomorrow,
      Promises nothing
      No epiphanies
      No paradise
      No utopia where

I'll be able to eat at the table
      without condescension and
      questions
      They'll wish me away
      or a way more
      appeasing
      They'll try to paint
      me them

When company comes
    I will curse them

Nobody'll dare
    look me in the eyes
    Too afraid to see
    a disappointed
    God
    Unwilling to

Say to me,
    I hear your song
    Instead   they'll offer
    smiles with clinched lips
    Their tears will drip as they
    pass the peas
    I will yell to them
"Eat in the kitchen,"

Then.
    I will curse them again
    in songs
    Dirges and anthems
    in their faces
    I will breathe in
    the breaths of queens
    the breaths of slaves
    the breaths of my grandparents
    and grandchildren
    and I will trumpet those breaths
    in song into their ears
    until they cup their hands at
    their face to collect the blood

Besides,
>   even if I sing
>   sweet and soft
>   angelic
>   serene
>   I doubt there'll be
>   a day seen when
They'll see how beautiful I am

>   So
>   I must see my own
>   beauty
>   Sing until my heart
>   remembers

And be ashamed –
>   of nothing
>   Not even the fact that
I, too, am America.

And The Walls Came Tumbling

Joshua fit de battle of Jericho, Jericho, Jericho
Joshua fit de battle of Jericho
An' de walls come tumblin' down.
Negro Spiritual

They will claim us rebels -
violations to the order of things.
We would not go quietly.
Our trumpets shook the rotted roots,
loosed grizzled grips clenching weathered reins.

Rain down, it did.
That wall, it did.
Our trumpets, not just blasting, but
beautiful like Satchmo,
like Miles,
like a Dizzying dirge,
like they play the best music at funerals.

They will paint us radical
and we will proudly drape ourselves in
revolution's rainbow.

Wail, it did.
That wall, did wail but we heard only
Negro spirituals and Native shouts and
Gumboot dancers rejoicing.

They will say nothing.
Rumble remains only under
the rubble of those walls.

And the walls came tumbling.

Acknowledgments

Ms. Elizabeth Bills, English and Creative Writing teacher at Boyd H. Anderson High School. You were the first to acknowledge my words as capable writing. Thank you for sparking the flame that became an obsession.

My ladies - Agnes, Triccilla, Takita, Na'Zyia, and Traniya. I have learned so much from each of you. You inspire me and give me constant material from which to draw from. And, Dae'kwon, you got a whole poem in the book, boy!

Omiokun Books. Thank you for choosing me for this journey. I am humbled and hope we sell a billion books.

Every student I've ever taught. Becoming a teacher made me a better person and writer. I am grateful to have served in the most important job there is, and I'm happy that I was only pushed so far and didn't end up in jail.

Shout out to the influences that are hip-hop, Saturday morning cartoons, elementary school gifted classes, Bible study, bullies, racism…and Marvin Gaye.

Darius V. Daughtry fell in love with words at the age of six. It was then, that he used to write and draw his own comic books. While the pictures left a little to be desired, being able to paint pictures with words was a passion that soon began to blossom. Darius has been marrying the pen to the paper ever since.

Today, Darius is an accomplished poet, playwright, director, educator and community builder who believes in the transformative power of words. As the Founder and Artistic Director of *Art Prevails Project*, a performing arts organization dedicated to expanding cultural conversation through performance, arts education, and community engagement, Darius works diligently to use the arts as vehicle for social change. As an educator, Darius has created and directed creative art initiatives, including some in conjunction with NFL Hall-of-Famer, Jason Taylor, and actor/poet, Omari Hardwick. His work has impacted thousands of youth throughout South Florida.

He continues to mentor many, and he loves his nieces.

You can drop him a line at info@dariusdaughtry.com.